DIAMONDS

DIAMONDS

POEMS BY

CAMILLE GUTHRIE

AMERICAN POETS CONTINUUM SERIES, NO. 189

BOA EDITIONS, LTD. ❖ ROCHESTER, NY ❖ 2021

First Edition
21 22 23 24 7 6 5 4 3 2 1

For information about permission to reuse any material from this book, please contact
The Permissions Company at www.permissionscompany.com or e-mail permdude@
gmail.com.

Publications by BOA Editions, Ltd.—a not-for-profit corporation under section 501 (c) (3) of the United States Internal Revenue Code—are made possible with funds from a variety of sources, including public funds from the Literature Program of the National Endowment for the Arts; the New York State Council on the Arts, a state agency; and the County of Monroe, NY. Private funding sources include the Max and Marian Farash Charitable Foundation; the Mary S. Mulligan Charitable Trust; the Rochester Area Community Foundation; the Ames-Amzalak Memorial Trust in memory of Henry Ames, Semon Amzalak, and Dan Amzalak; the LGBT Fund of Greater Rochester; and contributions from many individuals nationwide. See Colophon on page 88 for special individual acknowledgments.

Cover Design: Sandy Knight
Interior Design and Composition: Richard Foerster
BOA Logo: Mirko

BOA Editions books are available electronically through BookShare, an online
distributor offering Large-Print, Braille, Multimedia Audio Book, and Dyslexic
formats, as well as through e-readers that feature text to speech capabilities.

Library of Congress Cataloging-in-Publication Data

Names: Guthrie, Camille (Camille Suzanne), 1971- author.
Title: Diamonds : poems / by Camille Guthrie.
Description: Rochester, NY : BOA Editions, Ltd., 2021. | Series: American
    poets continuum series ; no. 189 |
Identifiers: LCCN 2021009569 (print) | LCCN 2021009570 (ebook) | ISBN
    9781950774456 (paperback) | ISBN 9781950774463 (ebook)
Subjects: LCGFT: Poetry.
Classification: LCC PS3557.U8477 D53 2021 (print) | LCC PS3557.U8477
    (ebook) | DDC 811/.54—dc23
LC record available at https://lccn.loc.gov/2021009569
LC ebook record available at https://lccn.loc.gov/2021009570

BOA Editions, Ltd.
250 North Goodman Street, Suite 306
Rochester, NY 14607
www.boaeditions.org
A. Poulin, Jr., Founder (1938–1996)

To my girlfriends

CONTENTS

I.

II.

III.

DIAMONDS

I.

VIRGIL, HEY

Ah me! I find myself middle-aged divorced lost
In the forest dark of my failures mortgage & slack breasts
It's hard to admit nobody wants to do me anymore
Not even Virgil will lead me down to his basement rental

Take a look at my firstborn son
Who put me on three months' bed rest
For whom I bled on the emergency room floor
Who declaims his device sucks
Stabs holes in his bedroom wall
Complains his ATV's too slow
Who plots to run away to join terrorists
He'd rather die than do math

And the little one ripped
From my womb in the surgery room
I pierced my nipples to unblock her milk
Who escapes from her car seat en route
Howls in rage 'cause her cake isn't pretty
Writes "No Mom" on her door with a Sharpie
Who says, "No fence but you're kinda fat"
She'd rather die than wear underpants

Virgil, hey! Send me down
To the second circle of hell where I belong
With those whom Love separated from Reason
Where an infernal hurricane will blast me
Hither & thither with no hope ever no comfort
Rather than drive these two to school this morning
And suffer forever with the other mothers

DIAMONDS

Judith Butler, I am calling you out
here in the kitchen where I'm unloading the dishwasher
performing my gender as I'm wont to do
My son yells from upstairs, How do you spell *probably?*
My daughter plays a game on my phone
caring for a little green monster who needs a bath
I need to buy diamonds so her monster can sing
I need a sack of diamonds so I can work part-time
and take care of my kids and still eat when I'm old
performing my old lady tasks
I hope I'm yarn-bombing an embassy somewhere
Better start learning to knit or whatever
Knitting performs femininity, apparently

We need diamonds to afford my house
now that I'm a single mom
conflict-free ones for a conflict-free life
To perform a single mom's gender
is to need a chest of gold coins
and my life is easy I am not hungry
not beaten up working three jobs taking night classes
not ill without insurance I have a good job
I'm already leveled up! Got all my privileges
I'm not floating on a raft to escape war
not having sex with soldiers for food
my children are not digging for diamonds
we're not being exploited in any way
"Could Be Worse!" is a book we love to read
at bedtime, it's by James Stevenson
It is, my son & I think, the plot to most movies
It is I think the plot to most lives

I'm lucky, I get to teach you, Judith
to students who eat up your words like candy hearts
who return to the arms of their friends
to dye their hair blue & fuck everyone & not shave
and make manifestos & tweet witty protests
who do drugs & sleep late & dance naked
They seem so unafraid ahistorical dreamfull
They stand outside the library smoking cigarettes
as if we're not going to die!
As if there aren't books to read!
I have the greatest job in the world
Could be a lot worse

But I'm lonely in debt there's no one to love me
I'm feeling sorry for myself & guilty for all my luck
Mutually contradictory states of mind
that's what Shakespeare invented, supposedly
Gender, you say, is a performance
continually created through *citational repetition*
Daily rituals we put on again & then again
as if we were born into a theatrical family
putting on the same play that's been going on forever
and there's no way out, so says Foucault
Michel, my turtle-necked darling, I love you
although you make me feel imprisoned
docile and subject to self-surveillance
Judith, Michel, I'm calling on you

I think I'm stuck in *Hamlet*
in the role of Queen Gertrude
but not at all royal I'm from Pittsburgh
because if I mention any man's name
my son says, I hate that guy
I asked him if he thought I was pretty
He said, Eh, you're okay-to-good

For his birthday he'd like a BB gun
My daughter spins in the living room to Rihanna
who has a pile of diamonds, probably
This little Ophelia talks to her Legos
and swims with water wings
She wants to know if music is air
She says my butt jiggles when I walk
Yes, that's it, I am a single Gertrude
in a little New England hamlet
Yet there are no louche kings to marry
no murderous uncles available nearby
Yet in the porches of my ear has poured
the poison of the wish for Reliable Love
Marriage's a prison
Then is the whole world one

What I want is someone, not a husband
to perform the male gender around my house
I need help stacking wood putting the garden to bed
for the winter I need a man in my bed
It goes way below zero in the winter round here
The garage door is broken I don't know how to fix it
Better learn to fix stuff, I guess
Like Gertrude, I am the Interpreter of the men around me
as I put snacks into little plastic bags
and so disciplined plan another play date
I play the Assuager I'm afraid
of being left with nothing for my future
No castle no bolthole on this dirty planet
No extra-small bag of gems
I have unappreciated skills, it's true
I know how to do a close reading
I know where commas go
I can spot phallogocentrism miles away
in my cat glasses I'm laying it down

Yet I'm terribly lonely, Judith
less lonely than Ophelia floating downstream
clutching flowers and singing sad songs

I want someone to perform love on me
Any kind of love any kind of role I don't care
but I want the real thing Real Love
To be a prisoner of Love, the songs say
and to perform all the sex acts, too
I want a masterful performance of that
with repeat performances
          Who's there?

I am sitting here folding laundry on the couch
performing the pairing of the socks
In anxiety and pleasure, you say
In the porches of my other ear
pours the poison of the wish for diamonds
Could be worse
My daughter spins her own tornado
My son builds a house of diamond blocks
I want the curtains to part now
I want to be swept away

DURING THE MIDDLE AGES

O God I am so fat
I cry all the time
A kitten scrubbed with a toothbrush online makes me sob
I'm so heartless seven species of bees
Are now endangered and I didn't do a thing
Didn't even send any money
To anybody doing any good
And I can't lose any weight I skipped yoga
I'm so hot all the time so broke
So pathetic no wise investments
Should've bought a 7-Eleven on a busy corner
When I was seven or eleven
Nobody wants to lick my neck
Nobody wants to hold my hand at the doctor's office
Nobody to grow old with me I'm so crabby
To pluck my beard feed the cat I don't have
And read me endless Russian novels at night
All the ones I still haven't got to so greatly depressing
Where are you handsome? Are you
Driving in your car to come visit me
Bringing a bottle of wine & a present so gallant?
A new translation of Akhmatova? I love it!

No? Well, I guess it's better than living
In the real Middle Ages when
Some shithead priest threatens you with hell
To pocket your last coin and there's no Tylenol
So you have to suck on some skullcap seeds
And knights canter about knocking you down
To take your maidenhood with pointy lances
And you have to work as a midwife with no birthing tub
Nobody washes their hands or votes

Nobody knows about DNA or PMS or NASA
There's nothing to read if you can read
Except boring doctrines or *Spiritual Exercises*
By Gertrude the Great, I'm not kidding
Yes, there's Dante Chaucer and some sagas
But it's not like you'd get near those books
You'd be lucky to have some jerk recite
The latest by Wulfstan the Cantor by campfire
Right before he beheads your uncles
And forces you to rub salve on his abs
You know you'd be sweating in a wheat field at twenty-two
Dying from your tenth pregnancy by the bailiff
Courtly love? Not a lot of it I bet

Some local doctor would have to drill a hole in my head
To let the demons out because I'd be full
Of black bile plus heresy as I am today
It would be an awfully hard time
When the sun revolves around the earth
And kings are unbelievably selfish
The Roman Empire fell flat
Vikings disemboweled your cousins
And the Lord of the Manor thinks you're cute
And it'll be a very long time before Pop Art
And meerkat videos and cotton candy
And sexting and fish tacos and girl bands
Everything's just so bad and you have buboes

Hopefully I'd get shoved into a nunnery
To have an ecstatic experience with mystical Jesus
Or better yet, I could be a hardcore samurai
Laying down justice on the heads of corrupt lords
But that was tough work, dirty work
You're working for nobility who at any period
In history are the worst people in the world

And to be an unemployed rōnin had to bite
Sunday afternoons no mom around to make you soup
Even if all the brothel ladies want to scrub your back
Sometimes you only want a nice nap
And some Neosporin on your wounds, ah

If only I could be like the divine Sei Shōnagon
Resplendent in silks with seven-layered sleeves
Writing in my room about politics, gossip, my lovers
Listing Splendid Awkward Annoying things
Things that Make One's Heart Beat Faster
I wish! Okay, I could be her devoted servant
Tidying her papers and fluffing her pillow
But even she found many hateful things
About living in the middle ages
Like crying babies messy guests and mansplainers
So irritating even way back then
You better shut up and take your medicine

MAGICAL OBJECT

It's a little-known fact
One of the most magical objects in the world
Is Sylvia Plath's prom dress
Strapless white duchesse satin
Full-skirted with a thousand layers of tulle
And a pleated heart-shaped bodice
I put it on
       I put it on
To cut an exquisite debutante silhouette
Because I need its power today
My marriage is over and my youth is gone
I need knowledge facility vision
And I don't want to drive into this tree
I zipped up the back by myself
And said, I want to live
       Pouf went the dress into a wide circle
Of vibrating luminous threads
Now I'm flying over my house
Where icy clouds blow over the roof
In a severe white winter sky
The sky is blue on Pluto I've read
Two hundred and thirty degrees below zero
Cold as the hearts of the enemies of poetry
       Nothing can pull down
The froth of this décolletage
As I hitch up the floor-length chiffon
My blue ankles peek from the hemline
As I soar over the ice fields of Pluto
Nothing can tear apart
These radiant waistline seams
       Plath knows what I mean
She who lived through the coldest London winter

Who wrote at night with chilled fingers
And made a rough decision
Her poems thrust from a scorched heart
Her line breaks slice through
      I put it on
My shoulders point above the glaring satin
To hold up the bodice my breasts fill out
The spotless tulle propels my body forward
Where are we going now, Plath?
What shall I do with your prom queen power?
Nobody nowhere can say

WISE WOMAN

Wise woman of Vermont, come out of the forest
Assure me I won't die lonely in these woods, show me
How to keep owls out of my hair, tell me how
To stack wood, to shoot trespassers, to seal the cracks
In my heart to keep the ice out, promise me
A catamount won't think I'm food
Make me a pot of venison stew
While you describe what to expect during the Changes
When you no longer sleep and my sorrow seems girlish
Teach me how to trim my whiskers when I get witchy
Advise me which mushrooms won't kill us quickly
Suggest stapling my kid to the wall till he's twenty-six
Tell me of your childless aunt who died asking for her kids
How do I make it in this cold hard land?
Tell me, where is the treasure buried?
What's the song I have to sing to myself?

GIRL TWIRLING

You orbit around a young star
In a rocket you travel to a pink planet
Fifty-seven light years from Earth
Four times the mass of Jupiter
Where no one will ever hurt you
No one will scare you
You hang upside down over the galaxy
You spin as fast as an electron
To the music you like in our living room
Where no one will grab your arm
Or tell you that you're dumb
No one will make you do something
You don't want to do
Unless it's time to go to school when
You sport a fedora and high-top Adidas
And wear a Totoro backpack
Dirt and candy smeared across your face
Your outflung arms create a force vector
Torquing our house into a whirl
This Dorothy makes her own tornado
No one will tell you things you already know
You know all the right words
Look into my eyes
My heart burns with righteous love
That's been on fire for 20 million years
I swear, if anyone ever looks at you weird
I will destroy them with one glance
I will remain nearby
In your residual scattered starlight

FAMILY COLLECTION

Art is a naked boy waiting for permission to move
High art is a twenty-dollar ticket times four
For me a friend and the kids to have an outing
A painting is a lush woman kneeling naked
Before us ripe breasts pushed forward
Pleased in her to-be-looked-at-ness
My daughter says, Yuck
Everything by Renoir displeases my friend
Who prefers the muddy world of Modernism
I tell my son to count how many naked people he sees
As we wander through the spacious galleries
Flesh captured in hushed brushy hues

Art is a French woman reading
Which I like because I like French novels and alone time
I would not like a man peering at me while I read Proust
An afternoon out is curried carrot soup with pepitas
A large salad of local feta and foraged fiddleheads
That my friend and I of twenty years share
Six-dollar grilled cheese for the kids with chips
Three-dollar sparkling waters also from France
My old friend smiles at me ironically
About all the bodies on display
Which bore the kids and she frowns
At *Slave Market* (1866) in which four men
Painted by Jean-Léon Gérôme examine
A nude young woman in a dingy courtyard
Her lit body faces us she wears a necklace
With one hand the man in the richest robes tilts
Her head toward him and with the other
Pokes two long fingers into her mouth
To test her teeth and her docility

The other women wait in a pile on the ground
A child squirms from their arms
A European "fantasy of rape" that allows
The viewer to frown upon faraway slavery
Outlawed in Europe by then, so says
The curator's note, and the worst detail
For me is that her pussy is bare

A day off takes two visits to the gift shop
To ponder if we need a puzzle of Van Gogh's face
Or a thirty-dollar rubber necklace in cerulean
An Impressionist apron or a Rembrandt tote
Fine art is a woman draped in a white cloak
Spreading a sail-like mantle over her face
She gazes down upon a silver censer
Burning the *Smoke of Ambergris* (1880)
Widely thought to be an aphrodisiac
A pale white wax that sperm whales vomit up
A fragrant bile duct secretion used in lotions and food
This I know from reading *Moby-Dick*
Alone in my bedroom with no man watching me
Or sticking his fingers into my mouth
Unless given explicit permission
Begun in Tangier and finished in Paris
Acquired by the museum in 1914
John Singer Sargent's model surely was a prostitute
The art historian says and quotes Henry James:
"I know not who this stately Mohammedan may be,
Not in what mysterious domestic or religious rite
She may be engaged; but . . . under her plastered arcade,
Which shines in the Eastern light, she is beautiful
And memorable." The historian explains that this mix
Of North African costumes and objects is a Western fantasy:
"The scene must be viewed as an imaginary one"
What captures me is the trajectory

Of her slender pinkie escaping
From the tip of her weighted hood and her calm arm
Vanishing into the complexity of her sleeve
What worries me is the grave silver necklace
Slung heavily across her breast
Orientalism to please the family who collected it
To enchant the visitors to their museum
Recently renovated for plenty-million dollars
For a relaxing afternoon to sit on the terrace
And walk through the sculptured grounds

I go out for a stroll with my kids
So my friend can take her time with the Van Goghs
A storm over a field has snatched her attention
The birds she later says hurt her feelings
Under the trees on the needled path
My son hurls rocks at tall trunks
My daughter follows the chipmunks
My thoughts fill up with the Rembrandt
Man Reading (1648) in its own dimly lit room
What thrills me is his thick index finger roughly
Stuck into the book to keep his place and the metal pin
Struck through his rumpled black jacket
And his riotous whiskers, which prove
That the exquisite exists in the particulars
Beneath his assertive dark hat
The man's left brow dips in concentration
His eyes focus on the warmly colored soft paper
His mouth quiet he is reading he is in another world
Rembrandt van Rijn's tender disgruntledness
Makes me feel wildly pleased I feel
Delighted to have been in its proximity
A few minutes to stare at a man reading
While my children get antsy and move on
Bored by the dull browns that say nothing to them

To me he says that life is utterly disappointing
Even if you are fucking Rembrandt
So you may as well read a good book
And for crying out loud
Be precise about whatever you do
I find it powerfully comforting
Since I'm middle-aged, crying, utterly disappointed
Divorced with a part-time job no savings
My future family collection made up of
My Little Ponies Warhammer guys Legos
And a Hilma af Klint poster I ordered from the internet
I love its humming blue pinwheel infinitude

I know not who I may be
Leaving with my two beautiful children
Who think I'm a bitch much of the time
I buy them a pricey rainbow of pencils
So I've done something right, but I keep thinking
As we drive home about *Snake Charmer* (c. 1879)
Also by Gérôme in which stands
A naked boy waiting neatly on a rug
Before a motley crowd huddled against
A wall in a blue-tiled room
Inspired by one in a palace in Istanbul
The stone floor like one in a Cairo mosque
With "a mishmash of clothing and weapons"
This boy who looks eight has seized
The attention of the onlookers by sporting
A thick snake wrapped round one shoulder
And his waist with one small hand he holds
Up the creature's head with the other its tail
Performing to the music of a seated boney flutist
The white-bearded leader glowers
As he lounges in his robes for the show
His long sword slung from his crotch

My friend had elbowed me and said,
That's literally the cover of *Orientalism*
Gérôme, certainly the dick of this collection
Traveled Egypt and "ensured his success"
By centering the soft butt of the boy

My kid tosses more rocks against the trees
On the path back to the museum
I'm scared they will ricochet and hit us
In the head we will be concussed
And not be able to look at any more paintings
My friend will have to drive us to the ER
I'm lucky we have family coverage
We won't be sent away we won't bleed internally
We won't be mishandled we won't be sold
I don't want my children to stand
Naked before a cruel man to be offered
To travelers for their pleasure
Or to rich people to be their servants or worse
Like the thousands of Syrian children
Gone missing in Europe
So says *The Guardian* online this morning
An unbearably cruel fact
"The scene must be viewed as an imaginary one"
Does not apply here
I read this news and go about my day
Taking my family on a lovely outing
I cannot bear for my children to be sad
To be slightly cold or the least bit hungry
Even if I am the worst one in their lives
Doing the most damage as mothers are said to do
I don't want them to be bored.

II.

MY NET WORTH

Two novels I haven't finished writing
Three strawberries in the garden that survived the chipmunks
Seven single earrings
An overgrown hydrangea outside the kitchen window
A bill for pink platform sandals
Six locally crafted beer bottles to recycle
One groundbreaking ode in the works
Longings for endowed and generous lovers with lots of time
Too much mint rapaciously growing
Plenty of prescriptions for the Pill, tick antibiotics, Xanax
Twenty-two years of teaching
Three vibrators, my favorite one's dying
Outline for a bestselling hilariously magical & tragic memoir
Eighties pop songs teeming in my head
Shattered Dreams, So Emotional, Don't You Want Me
Several serious arguments I'd like to have and win
Imaginary comebacks and devastating last words
A few pretty patterned throw pillows to throw
A house I can't afford on fourteen acres of woods
Plowing bills, mowing bills, seasoned gourmet firewood bills
A barn full of dusty books, something chewed *The Portrait of a Lady*
Daydreams of literary glory and glorious revenge
Fantasies of being friends with Roland Barthes and Joan Jett
A pond full of muck and one snapping turtle
Debts to my parents, mostly emotional
No savings, no loans, no liens
No securities, no offshore accounts, no sex tapes
Two cesarean scars
One small hernia from coughing for a month
A worthless wedding ring
Purple bruises from Nerf hatchet play
Two unicorn tattoos, temporary

One tick bite behind my ear, somewhat swollen
A slipped disc from sitting at desk worrying over poems
Persistent crying jags, driving back and forth to soccer practice
Scratched oversized sunglasses from the outlet
Many girlfriends available 24/7 for complaining
Anxious insomnia and tooth grinding
Perimenopausal Klingon rage and bloating
Sagging breasts from nursing forever
Cavities, pockmarks, varicose veins
A battered unrealistically hopeful heart
Poems by Emily Dickinson in my ear
I cannot live with You—
Three hundred and forty-seven dollars

I AM GIVING UP POETRY

But he that writes of you, if he can tell
That you are you, so dignifies his story.
                              —Sonnet 84, Shakespeare

I am giving up poetry for kissing you, I mean it
When your body nears mine, metaphors are tedious nitpickers
Similes as useless to me as an IUD from the seventies
I don't want representation I want to make out in parking lots

When you touch my breasts, sonnets are painfully brief
Epics dull and long, too many battles, I long to be alone with you
For just an hour, no allusions to Yeats, just your weight on mine
There's no subtlety to my intentions, no puns, no ambiguity

There's no time for rhymes! The ice shelves have slid into the sea
Total hive collapse, don't you know I want to embrace you
Not ennobling truths? I don't want prizes or to be read by future girls
My words mean only what they say, this is my New Realism

It's not very political yet it's urgent and you are you
I have critical work to do like licking your sweet face

MY BOYFRIEND, JOHN KEATS

We walk hand in hand through the museum
We are at the Met in September
So you're emotional, we stroll
Carelessly through the hall of antiquities
You whisper to the statuettes
"Fill all fruit to ripeness"
They won't answer you, darling
I pull you close and glare at the gallery guard
Hush, John, calm yourself and focus
I am your sylvan historian
I am your bride of quietness
We will make a foster child of silence
Here? you ask, English and polite
Yes, here by the *Terracotta Bucket*
Later, we are back in my bedroom
Enough, Keats, with the formal foreplay!
You cry that you're still in love with Fanny
Do not say that name, I cannot bear being haunted
By Miss Brawne in her hand-sewn outfits
My love, let me remind you
I have The Beatles, Nina Simone, The Goldberg Variations
You may waste mellow hours with headphones on
And I will send you pics of me naked
Your dark eyes will be riveted to artifice
Fanny doesn't have what you need
Fanny doesn't have antibiotics
Fanny doesn't tweet to the skies
Fanny wears a bonnet
Keats, what are you doing
Sitting in a moss'd tree—having thoughts?
Are you inventing immortal lines?
It's time for lunch, it's sushi takeout

Do not sink in a heap, John Keats
You are tubercular and five-foot-one
Here is your new fleece jacket
Here is a bowl of hot oatmeal
And a cup of PG Tips with milk
Sit here by the leaf-fringed window
And wrap yourself in this scarf
I bought it on Etsy, I'm not Fanny
Let me run you a bubble bath
        I love you, small Keats
Wake up, John, it's a bad dream
There's no mad pursuit, no cows led to slaughter
Your dryad's right here, shopping online
For organic flannel sheets to keep you cozy
I'll be your nightingale in the darkling night
I'll read you Homer till you fall asleep
Put your laden head on my shoulder
Bold Lover, that's you!
Haunt about this shape, Keats
Tease me out of thought
I will not fade, I will have your bliss
Forever wilt thou love, and I am fair
Fanny won't tie you up, I can
Fanny can't make your poems go viral, I can
I can drive you straight to the ER
To save you & Romantic Poetry forever
You know that guy who kept your inheritance?
I stabbed him through the heart with a pencil
The critics who said you were working class?
Dead—quills through their eyeballs
And Wordsworth, who condescended to you?
Choked by my own bare hands
It was easy, I hate Wordsworth
They won't bother you again, go ahead
Continue working on your odes

Honey, I summoned your beloved mother
I brought back your brothers from the dead
How? With my love powers
To resurrect you through space and time
Don't try to climb out the window
Please pay attention, John Keats
Now let me cure you
We don't want you to die at twenty-five
We love you and your sad poetry!
I have first-class tickets to Rome
We will visit the Vatican and eat gelato
We will kiss in an outdoor café
The warm days will never cease
My love, we will not visit your grave

SERIOUS MOONLIGHT

Serious moonlight fell brightly on the mountains tonight
Elegant moonlight fell loudly on the deer asleep in the yard
Broken moonlight fell splendidly on the swing set
Moody moonlight fell hard on the weedy pond

Pretty moonlight fell recklessly on the garden beds
Cruel moonlight fell on the car parked in the driveway
Fierce moonlight fell thoughtlessly on the recycling bins
Actual moonlight fell wildly on the coyotes falling on a rabbit

Personal moonlight fell intentionally on my desk and books
Ancient moonlight fell perfectly on the bedsheets
Modern moonlight fell roughly scattering my thoughts
Bowie died last night his exquisite alien soul has taken off

You are with another and I'm falling repeatedly
Shattered by this silently falling terrible moonlight

VICTIM OF LOVE

It may be true
that I'm limerent
for you another victim
of love I've got all
the relevant symptoms

At the Dairy Bar waiting
for fries I see you
lunching with a friend
mood-dependent I'm ready
to pour vats of ketchup
onto her head, yet when
you say hey I order
rainbow sprinkles
for everybody

I remember every bit
of how you explained
the ancient trade routes
so cute! I tried concealing
my need to sob into
your shoulder to disguise
my longing for reciprocal
feelings—denied

Oh, you know that Tuesday
you pressed me hard
up in the hallway below
the Manet print and kissed
me till Doomsday and promised
me true love halfway? That's
a day I often replay

The tears haven't ceased
because you didn't invite me
to watch a John Candy movie
but you asked Lucie and Abby I
hate you I hate every lady
ever born I hate everything
from the eighties I'm going
to run a film fest of Italian
revenge films from the sixties
and not invite you especially
not Abby nor Lucie

Like a tween the moment
Zayn left the band
my love's intensified by
adversity like when
you left for a seaside vacation
and never sent one
postcard I cried so badly

Oversensitive to random
interactions I hope to bump
into you at the Rite Aid
that shampoo and shaving cream
in your basket quite attractive
I want action in the aisle of lotions
Who are the condoms for?
Me? Better be

Sometimes you pass me by
in your little rusted-door car
your quick wink at
the stop sign fills
me with religious
adoration

Upon waking much
aching in the heart
at four in the morning
snow's coming down hard
I'm aging alone
online dating's
not for the weak
I'd rather be mating
for life like prairie voles but
you're ice-skating arm-in-
arm with a waitress it's just
degrading heartbreak

My feminist friends
think I'm insane
to wait for you
endlessly my nemesis
at yoga thinks you
merely feign interest
Even my therapist so patient
when I complain says,
Do we need to
talk about this again?

There's an election
Presidential there are wolves
moving south from the ice melt
floods left Louisiana
a disaster area dire world
affairs but tonight you
brought bubbly wine
and called me honey
I am walking on air

LOVE, MADAME DU BARRY

Dear King Louis XV,
Today I borrowed your sleigh
Carved like a green dragon with golden wings
Sat my butt on the velvet *chinois* seat
And took off led by your best black pony

I dropped by that blonde upstart from Italy
Who sported a carousel in her hair
In a plot to wreck me at the marionette theatre
And stole my loyal glove-maker
I left some bonbons on her doorstep
She won't get up for two weeks

You know the dark-eyed Duchess from Denmark?
She tried to blackmail me with drawings from my past
I went round to her new place by the Seine
Said, That move's going to cost you
Better run home to your rich papa
I know about you and the help
No girl, heave that inflated bosom north

From a traveler I met at the menagerie
I tested a secret weapon from the East
On the silky black-locked beauty from Belgium
No, not her sister—the one who smells of cheese
Who slandered me in a gutter pamphlet
Her doctor says the rash's incurable, it's too bad
She won't be at your croquet party Saturday

My hairdresser told me everything
So I had to rub out that long-lashed Swiss slattern
That's the last we'll see of her country cute

Go back to milking goats, sweetie
And take that Irish adventuress with you
They say she's handy in a stable

Yeah, I dusted that dull tart from Germany
With the flouncing walk and ten-inch waist
I knew of her treachery from the start
Set up a long ride to nowhere with my entourage
Mädchen Munchkin won't know what hit her

I made a stop at Rue de Foie Gras
To bump off that ruffled drama trap from Amsterdam
Commissioning nudes of yourself? Please
That's so 1768, so tired of her machinations
She had the nerve to touch my diamonds

You are walking perfection, God's gift to France
I do love your new perfume from the Indies
Do you have any more of those little boys?
The one you gave me brings me
A cup of chocolate every morning at nine sharp
Asking for a friend

At the casino where I was formerly embedded
I had tea with our mutual friend
Sure, he rescued me from caring for the elderly
Selling trinkets on the streets and part-time haberdashery
But you try servicing all the ministers in one weekend
Who does he think he's talking to?
I glide in royal circles now

My love, in case you were fretting
I neutralized that horrid Infanta
Little baby won't be following you around
And whining in corridors anymore, boring!

I found her a luxurious convent in the Alps
Let me get her a straw

Darling, why not pass on
Your precious genes to me?
Put me and junior up in an empty pavilion
I'm still fertile though I'm 25
Marie, Princess of Poland? Is that her name?

The villagers were blown away by my sleigh
I clipped a peasant by the way
A small one, *Zut! Alors!*
I just don't fucking know anymore
I'm uncertain of the future

A MAN OF LEGEND

I.

Remember when you were tutor to Nero?
You burned so hot in your linen robes
That soul patch Wayfarers and sarcastic wit
He blamed you for the Great Fire of Rome

II.

Merchant sailors tell tales of your beach body
Sing of the battle when you head-banged a kraken
Its tears drowned an atoll
That was a sad day in Old Oceania

III.

Nine medieval volumes dedicated to your cheekbones
Ten thousand Latin lines concern your swagger
Three out of four monks sweated over the verbs
Painstakingly transcribing your butt in bike shorts

IV.

This 10th-century Byzantine encyclopedia relates
Your early training with imperial masters
Master of kickboxing, archery, Bulgarian raiding
And sixteen arts of seduction, whew! I'm spent

V.

The Seven Sages of Greece prophesied
The Bulge of His Biceps in a 12,000-line poem
12,000 graduate students are decoding it daily
No one will survive or graduate on schedule

VI.

Neither fire nor flood nor neglect nor bookworms
Can touch the Legacy of the Moneymaker
Or misinterpret the Epic of Your Bits at this moment
I'm retranslating the original manuscript

WORKS & DAYS

Poetry doesn't make you any money
Everybody's been telling me since forever
Well, I get to sit in a classroom with sweetie pies
And discuss how Shakespeare abuses metaphors
You can go bonus shopping island hopping card swiping
On a themed cruise with Captains of Industry
Those guys don't make me swoon

Today I don't want to send my poems out
To be rejected I want to stay in bed
And daydream of writing lines sharp as Sontag's
Everybody says, Don't work all the time
So let subtle truths fret elsewhere
I want you here in my warm arms
When I'm done reading, that is

On workdays meaning must be fisked out
A shining particle pried from an ancient geode
This afternoon I prefer to sit in your lap
Bury my face in your chest hair
Fragrant as a fairy-tale forest or something

Get to my house early in the morning
Eye contact is our only task
A trail of ionized light lingering between us
And press your scruff cheek to mine
Stop it with the I-have-to-go-to-work-now
It's not nice when we are capable of infinity
So what if we end up impoverished & unpublished
Let's strive for perfection

III.

BE MORE LIKE BJÖRK

First sew yourself into a pom-pom mushroom
Stride across the thirstland past faerie lights
Shout complaints inside volcanic mancaves
Scout for the last unlocated spring of ylem
Then plait a cottage out of kestrel fluff
Stir potato eyes into a vat of dislocated feelings
Write a luculent novel five winters long
Till dismay ferments enough nuclear energy to power
Your moon buggy beyond the nacaret fields
Then plunge over cliffs sporting moth wings
Dropping to the bottommost of the besprinkled sea
And make your way up through the rain shadow
On two cat feet into hostile territory
All the while you compose a callithumpian song
To nail the spot-on ritual within the astrobleme
So bend dragons and constellate your enemies
Fox on your shoulder spend a month sun-grazing
A hundred hawks exploding before your gait
Which will bring you luck on this godawful day
You must make a new life by yourself
Like all lurching tellurians stuck in eviternity

A YOUNG DAUGHTER OF THE PICTS

To Do

Strut around the shire like I'm all that in my new flower tattoos.

Linger near the travelers from Northumbria to catch up on Seven Kingdom gossip, casually holding my spear in case they get mouthy.

Give the side-eye to that Angle hussy showing off her pelts like no one ever skinned a wild boar before.

Why does everyone hanging out in a *broch* have to sing all the time? Can't a girl have a little quiet in a *crannog*?

Bury everyone east of the Forth-Clythe isthmus in the cattle-breeding contest this fall.

Promise the Viking tied up in my hut that he can return north to his mama if he obeys my every word.

From my secret cove on the coast, swim way out. Relax in the Viking's boat. Comb hair out in the sun.

Paint my face with woad and leap out at that newcomer, Ninian, when he comes back from that altar he's building. Press foot on his face until he shuts it. Tell him: I'd rather tattoo *Pagan* across my face than convert to what he's selling.

Wonder, while I'm milking my goat, why we have kings when we insist upon matrilineal succession? Pat her flanks fondly, gaze at the distant green hills.

Invite the new witch over, the one who makes good mead. Stay up late talking about stuff and teasing the Viking with our braids.

Build a bonfire to send signals to the Romans. I hear they have cool haircuts.

Strangle that hermit with my tresses if he steals from my nettle patch again. If I don't have a cup of tea in the morning, I'm irritable.

Make out with that Gael fellow if I get bored. Ah, that bushy beard! Meat & milk, those bulging thighs!

Ninian says Roman women can't do this and can't do that. Just try to take my spear from me. Just because you can build aqueducts doesn't give you the right.

The Viking wastes his mornings knitting me a wool sweater. Do I look like I'm cold? Idiot.

Get some sand between my toes. Why don't I take a boat and float south to see what the Britons are up to? That would be something different.

Order a double-ringed metal choker for the human sacrifice next month.

When I'm hiking with my dog, Hero, I want to be alone. When I'm making leek soup, I don't like to share. When I go to bed, I like to ride a Viking.

Inform Ninian that he smells like cabbage. Enjoy his discomfort. That's what he gets for insulting my polytheism.

Sharpen spear. Consider revenge on the Angles of Bernicia, who need to be reminded who's boss.

Spit from the top of the cliff. Ponder clouds. The insignificance of it all. Ponder if pirates will come this way. Ponder becoming Pirate Queen.

Ninian waited for me when I was out gathering wild garlic. He said his god said he could fondle my ass. I said my gods said you better not fall into this here wolf trap.

In a swap—boar jerky for a vision—the witch warned me of things to come: Christianity, Colonialism, Cops, Capitalism. A sad, terrible future.

Force the Viking to build me a fabulous funeral boat. Preparing ahead.

For good luck, paint pebbles with some pentacles and crescents. Pass out charm stones at the goat roast this weekend. It can't hurt.

Find a worthy pirate. Birth a new nation.

UPON READING MILTON

How shall I part and whither wander down
Into a lower world, to this obscure
And wild, how shall we breathe in other air
Less pure, accustomed to immortal fruits?

—*Paradise Lost*, Book XI, John Milton

Students say *Say-in* when they read *Paradise Lost*
White girls from Catholic schools whither wander down
Good daughters forever long for the obscure and wild

Whichever way he flies the Lord of Darkness needs a hard *T*
I long to meet that blank verse to breathe its other air
But his daughter, Deborah, forced scribe, gets in my way

He turned her out & her sister, too, for his third wife
Happiness at last after the divorce tracts and Civil War
Two wives dead on the blood-soaked birthing bed

Blind Milton worked his great poem in a green suit and sword
Made his daughters milk his grand ambivalence
They sold some of his books, he didn't understand why

My dreams long for no tyrant shouting from a cloud-ship
Stuck in this lower world, I want this dented red apple
Less pure and plucked from a child's plastic grocery cart

THE IDEAL FORM

I've found it
What Plato said
From the Winter 2006 Collection
A dusty rose 100% silk knee-length
Pleated trim at neck pin-tucking at bodice
Low scoop over the breast self-tie bow
Concealed back zip closure no pocketed
Valentino dress "Condition Pristine"
Estimated retail $5,238 online
Bust 28" Waist 25" Hip 32" Length 39"
Made in Italy, made for me today
It's the Form of the Dress

It's not a sundress not a shirtdress
Not a mini not a maxi not a wrap
No pouf no halter no spaghetti straps
Not a bubble blouson or ball gown
Not one-shoulder not tiered not A-line
Not Grecian Empire or Sabrina
Not a tent not apron definitely not Bodycon
Not a jumper prom tunic or maid
Not shift sheath slip

It's an utterly perfect light pink dress
To wear to be my perfect self
In this imperfect corrupt world
Maybe my prom dress had a 25" waist
Before motherhood before my forties
When I was Condition Pristine

I need the Perfect Form now
To wear to this meeting today

To finalize the end of my marriage
I need all the power of the history of femininity
The indignation of every wife ever
Who has been left without $5,238 to participate
In one of the world's finest ideas
The Form of Beauty
"Itself by itself with itself" says Plato
Which makes us all insane
Living as we do in Late Capitalism
All alone online late at night scrolling
For the perfect date perfect body perfect outfit
Unaffordable and perfectly devastating
To make everyone in the room
Gasp from its spectacular beauty
And you win even though
Now you enter a room by yourself
Into this dangerous world of shadows
Without a way without the means
To the perfect dress and to go with it
Perfect fuck-you heels

DATING PROFILE

Who I am: Hieronymus Bosch

What's happening in my life now: I'm looking for the perfect match to share the so-called earthly delights.

What I know how to do: I'm good at flying by winged trout, navigating only with a cherry—sporting armor and a merman tail. I'm known to take an afternoon dip with my head buried in sand, while I balance a mushy raspberry—impaled by a blue branch and sat upon by two birds mulling lunch—between my thighs, and covering my privates, of course. I'm not bad at dangling nude from a giant marriage ring, the one slung round the spear piercing the Double-Testicle Tower apartments, while crystalline pneumatic tubes spit forth flocks of blackbirds.

What people often say about me: I ride goldfinches with a gleaming tear on my head for a helmet. They say I nap face-down in public parks purely to entice deer to sniff my freckled bare back. Both true. It's said that I dated a lugubrious lady and together we floated in a gutted peach with our pets (her heron and my butterfly) showing off our houseplants until my leg protruded rudely from one side and sank us—also correct. People also say I frequent the ape cave deep in a diseased blackberry for s'mores, but it's a lie.

What I like: I like flanged mermaids who flirt with anonymous knights, visors down, both terminating piscinely. I enjoy an embrace with a blank-eyed owl, wider than an armoire, when wading in a birth canal. I like to drift in an overripe fruitboat sprouting a dandelion trap from one end that has captured a bubble about to burst from the weight of the naked couple it cradles, and from the other end, pokes a chemist's tube for observing a shy jerboa. I suspect she is a sex doll—the woman, not the rodent. I confess that I'm fond of extra-large cherry kebobs if served by spoon-billed waiters.

What I can't live without: I have to say family. To our weekly barbecue, I wear an elderberry fascinator and watch my father's silver face silently shouting beneath a soldier's helmet, which thrusts forth a clenched hand from leg armor where his ear should hang. Across the table, my mother, a sparrow-colored fish in rainboots with a rat's head, chews a plate of salamander chips like there's no tomorrow. Herons perched upon their heads, my twin sisters arrive in time for dessert to regale us with tales of their lifeguard shift at the Virgins-Only pool. We stroll in the neighborhood afterwards, waving to the teapot army led by the pissed-off trout captain with moth ears who marches to the end of the world.

What's on my mind lately: Do you think at the Last Judgment you will be straddled by a hedgehog who needs a haircut, shield shining on his back, as he neatly slices your arm off, and concurrently a pelican-rat gnaws on your armpit? In Hell, will you hold hands with a thrush buttoned into a cardigan and tight jeans and listen all night to the tunes of a bagpipe made from a giant's bladder? At the end of days, will your ears detach from your head and inflate to couple with an arrow, rolling forward tank-sized to crush the frantic masses for miles, whilst hugging an ogre's dagger? As the world burns, will you desolate on the porch of a reptile egg with that fiery crew gambling in the rear of the Tree-House-Man who crouches in rowboats, while a troubled moth loiters at the bottom of your ladder, and, at the same time, the gray-hooded man inexorably climbs toward you, shouldering a hockey stick that draggles pottery, a feathered dart jutting from his ass? Or, will you idly flatulate ravens?

What I'm usually doing on a weekend night: Fridays, I'm the kind of guy who will hoist a human-sized jackrabbit onto my back and

crash my neighbor's varicose-veined egg house party. Streaming
eternal music all night long from sphere-tipped florescent steeples,
we love to dance on the roof with engorged green pearls on our
heads or be beak-fed by a massive duck. On Saturdays, I'll show
up at the hollowed-out blueberry bash, showing off my behind
or getting a hug, hanging out all prelapsarian, until we range in
packs searching for divine snacks. Inviting everybody back into
my sublet, a busted embryo, after some refreshing laps in juice
runoff, is also cool. You know what's fun? Sitting cross-legged
with my nude co-workers to worship a lush whortleberry big as a
Volkswagen. Most holiday weekends though, I strap on my fruitlet
backpack and take a hike alone, distracted by thoughts of tattooing
a melody on my butt or fretting that I might be crucified on a
harp.

What I'm willing to admit: Once I dated an Eve, her gilded hair
falling like a fleece blanket to her ankles, and I clung to her like a
besotted amphibian. One evening in our favorite café, she dumped
me for a constellated cape-wearing, torch-carrying dragon, who
stomped pirate-like through the reckoning and away with my
future. Indifferent to my feelings, a pot-bellied monkeyman
strummed a lute on his head to accompany the flute-nosed,
dragoon-booted upright plesiosaur rapping into the open mike.
What still hurts is the orange-hatted, centipede-tailed, pope-
headed maître d' on frog feet, his ears plugged by plates, who stood
and stared as my heart ripped open like a swollen gooseberry, and
its pet crane abandoned the apex of my hopes.

You should write to me if: You would like to meet me at the
crenellated pink cathedral on Eden pond—the one with the
petal-fluted spire and the electric water splurting from its fallopian
fountains where peacocks roost. In its pimpled nave dwells a
concerned owl. I'll take you there on my flying gryphon, who
clutches a confused bear, so that we can pretend to be flexible
zookeepers. Don't fear, I steer with a frothy tree and my co-pilot

is a self-possessed kestrel. Upon landing at Sapphire Jelly Island, we can practice headstands—your head balanced perfectly on mine—while I do twenty naked squats on an erect mushroom. My roommates won't bother us—they're too busy scissoring strawberries, or training otters for the mammal parade, or debating in a crab cornucopia about the human condition, and, finally, patting each other's nether regions from which bouquets spring.

COME BACK!

Hey H.D., come back, there's trouble all over
Ruins, as you said, there, as here
I need your flowering vision, lady
Come with your angels and blank book
With your elegant cheekbones
Your loquent lines upswept white hair
Lyrical long fingers and dark wool cape
As I'm reading the news

Help us, we filled the oceans
With the plastic crap we like to buy
Choked the sea-nymphs, let loose toxins into the sky
The land is parched, the poles are melting
My friends are canning food and buying guns
I have serious doubts, I have two children
You had one, Perdita, the Lost One
We live in the country and drank water
Poisoned by a chemical factory nearby
So people could eat microwave popcorn
And make omelets with nonstick pans
It's not that bad, our blood levels are so-so
It's my job to protect them, H.D.
From bullies traffickers warmongers
I will write down everything you say

When bombs fell around your family
You seemed so sure in your poems
Walking down a London street
Thinking of Egypt of Mary of ruins
You stepped through a broken wall to see
A bomb-blackened apple tree flowering
It guided you through the Blitz

Here when cherry blossoms appear after the winter
I think, Pretty pink ladies
Don't catch a disease and die on us

I remember the Two Towers falling
People pulverized into clouds of dust
We breathed in their particles
A sickly sweet smell smoldering for months
That week the skies bore a blue clarity
What can you teach me now?
I don't think the petitions I'm signing are helping
Not religious have no husband need advice

Where to now, H.D.?
Come near, if you can bear it
I know, it's not exactly here as there
We have made our own problems
Aloud I read your poems and there
You stand at the top of the stair
Holding your book, your cape falls over me
H.D., tell me what to do

TO BRING YOU NEWS

I.

Great news! A hiker found in a broken clay pot
The complete, unexpurgated works of Sappho
I made a plectrum from your eyelashes
Somebody somewhere will stroke a lyre in tribute

II.

The troops of Caesar didn't burn the library of Alexandria
To save it a million librarians pushed it into the Mediterranean
From our bed we can browse its 700,000 scrolls online
Who plunged Europe into the Dark Ages? Not us

III.

We spotted the Dark Lady of the sonnets
Sporting tit windows and pleather hot pants
She nailed "Barracuda" on karaoke night
If you don't clap, she'll steal your man
And put your head on a spike on London Bridge

IV.

Milton is not for lovers in this postlapsarian world
Everybody gets punished, and it's no fun at all
Angels lecture and men labor and complain about it
Women suffer at men's hands and die in childbirth
Nobody gets to say they're sorry or make a joke

V.

If you want to be ravished by God, fine
But that impotence better be metaphysical, mister
We're so over the 17th century
No time for your closets or conceits
No room for your paradoxes and backtalk
We want to own property and vote

VI.

The Lake Poets paddle quite nicely
Do you think Coleridge was a fiend in bed
Especially when high & talking Shakespeare?
Shelley? Maybe a passive-aggressive Bottom
The worst, Wordsworth, a joyless Top
Blake? Bedding an angel never works out well

VII.

Such fetishists & shabby poets
The Pre-Raphaelite Brotherhood we admit was hot
I'm going to drown them all with my lush red hair
Then choke a knight with my bosom
I will need antibiotics after that frat house

VIII.

Doesn't anybody read Modernism anymore?
H.D.! Langston! Mina! Zora!
Please lay your fine visions before us
I don't want anyone else intoning at me
Lightly I step my sandals over the footnotes

IX.

Feeling sorry for the Confessionals lately
How many epiphanies can one have in a day?
Gosh, it's exhausting & suicide's not sexy anymore
Nor are asylums or alcoholic rages
I want to ride off on Ariel into the future

X.

I hung up my underpinnings in public
Constructed an ironic simulacrum
Post-poetry post-human post-time
Yet the real prevails
The sea level rises idealism falls
And ruthless ideologies abound
Put your head down
We have serious work to do

BEAUTIFUL POETRY

The poem is you.
—"Paradoxes and Oxymorons," John Ashbery

I was too shy to say anything except, Your poems are so beautiful
What kinds of things, feelings, or ideas inspire you
I mean, outside the raw experiences of your life?
He turned a strange crosshatched color
as if he stood in an overcast painting, and said, Oh, thanks
yet no other phenomena intrude upon my starlit mind

I see you are wondering what this is all about. Don't mind
me, I'm talking to myself again. Yes, poetry is nice and often beautiful
but it doesn't beget much attention, money, or even a simple thanks
for placing the best words in the best order. That's when I forget all about
    your
incessant demands, and the restless subject leaps the stream in
    Technicolor—
until the Remembrancer appears and says, Stop this wasteful life

Doctor, lawyer, thief. These fancies of yours could cost a life
or worse, two. Meanwhile, he perceives my gifted body upholding my
    mind
as I'm explaining my stuff on the *Unicorn Tapestries*, cheeks starting to
    color,
feathers ruffling, quiet shudders. He shrugs, That sounds too beautiful
but I'd like to read it sometime. He says all the right things, like I love
    you
Hyacinth Girl. Things get interesting until the sudden blow: Thanks

For the memories. What I think seeing his work in *The Paris Review* is
    thanks
for nothing! As he drops me for that prolific pastoral life
with his wife upstate. The more I think about it, it all depends upon your
phantom attention. Surely a world embroiders itself in one's mind

at any moment, words resounding ardent present clarifyingly beautiful
and beautifully truthful. You know? Here I could put in a lapis lazuli
    color

Or a murky midnight blue. Or have the crowd stagger by in a riot of
    color
pinning down the helpless beast with spears and ritualistic thanks
to their gods. What one wants to get at is the real, the eternally
    beautiful
like *The White Album* or something. That's what makes one's perilous life
worth living. All the brute indifference, humiliation, and failure can put
    one in mind
to give up, freak out, heart-battered, so mastered. Oh you

Wherever I go, on the subway, at work, at play, in sleep, it's always you
of the air, overpowering my senses like a Dutch master in one pure color
its fiction at full speed, walls breaking, a clarity panorama for the mind
hunting for meaning and finding it at last! Now look at all the work I
    did, and not one thanks—
not even flowers. Off you rush to watch him accept another award in
    that life
I can only dream of. From where you sit it all seems so beautiful

And I finally understand you. For that I can't express enough thanks
as the subject is the best color for me in the difficulty of this lonely life.
It's always caught up in my mind, and what could be more beautiful.

NOTES

"Virgil, Hey" alludes to Canto I of Dante's *Inferno*, the Longfellow translation: "Midway upon the journey of our life / I found myself within a forest dark, / For the straightforward pathway had been lost. // Ah me! how hard a thing it is to say." I also refer to a poem by T'ao Ch'ien (365–427 CE) called "Scolding My Children," which begins: "My temples covered all in white, I'm / slack-muscled and loose-skinned for good // now" (translated by David Hinton in 2000).

The italicized parts in "Diamonds" refer to Judith Butler's essay "Performative Acts and Gender Constitution: An Essay in Phenomenology and Feminist Theory" (1988), in which she writes this fine sentence: "The authors of gender become entranced by their own fictions whereby the construction compels one's belief in its necessity and naturalness." James Stevenson wrote *"Could Be Worse!"* in 1987.

In "During the Middle Ages," I mention Sei Shōnagon (c. 966– c. 1025), who wrote in "Hateful Things" from *The Pillow Book (Makura no sōshi)*: "A man who has nothing in particular to recommend him discusses all sorts of subjects at random as though he knew everything" (translated by Ivan Morris in 1967).

"Magical Object" was inspired by reading that Smith College Library keeps Sylvia Plath's prom dress in their archives.

"Wise Woman" is dedicated to Ann Fitzgerald with many thanks to the Southshire Community School, Coleen Healy, and its community.

The paintings I describe in "Family Collection" are *Slave Market* (1866) and *Snake Charmer* (c. 1879) by Jean-Léon Gérôme; *Smoke of Ambergris* (1880) by John Singer Sargent; and the marvel, *Man Reading* (1648) by Rembrandt van Rijn, all from The Sterling and

Francine Clark Art Institute's collection. I quote Henry James and commentary from art historian and curator Steven Kern from the Clark Art Institute's website.

"My Net Worth" contains the first line of Emily Dickinson's poem "I cannot live with You—" (1863).

"My Boyfriend, John Keats": I have learned that biographers of John Keats often dismiss and ridicule his love, Fanny Brawne. I have also noticed how competitive some poets I know—including myself—are about how much we love Keats.

"Serious Moonlight" is, of course, a lyric from David Bowie's song "Let's Dance" from the album of the same name (1983).

Many thanks to Ananda Brutvan who explained to me the concept of limerence, which appears in "Victim of Love."

"Love, Madame du Barry" is my response to Robert Browning's "My Last Duchess." Upon visiting the Montreal Museum of Fine Arts, I came upon a French sleigh shaped like a dragon (c. 1720–1750) attributed to the court of Louis XV: a spectacular, Orientalist object that I imagined the king's mistress, Madame du Barry, might use to visit her rivals for his royal attention.

Among many exorbitant presents, including an outrageous diamond necklace, King Louis XV bought du Barry a child—Zamor (1762–1820), a boy of Bengali or Siddi origin, whom British slave traders trafficked from Chittagong. Madame du Barry insisted that he was African and ordered him to bring her a cup of chocolate every morning. Disgusted by her and her extravagance, Zamor later joined the Jacobins and informed on du Barry, leading to her eventual trial and beheading during the Reign of Terror.

The vocabulary in "Be More Like Björk" came from a list of archaic words I read by chance online.

"A Young Daughter of the Picts": This miniature painting (c. 1585) preoccupies me because of its many incongruities: its willful misreading of history, its fantasy about colonialism, and its ornamentation of the female body. Confusion about its painter adds to the strange anachronism of this Daughter, who, to me, resists exactitude.

At first it was attributed to John White (c. 1540–c. 1593), a mapmaker and artist, who accompanied Richard Grenville, the British admiral sent to establish a military colony on Roanoke Island, inhabited by the Carolina Algonquins. In 1585, Grenville infamously killed the Aquascogoc people when a silver drinking cup went missing from his belongings. White sketched and painted watercolors of the indigenous people and the landscape; eventually, he became the governor of the "Lost Colony" and grandfather to the first English child born in the Americas, Virginia Dare. White's drawings were included in Theodorus de Bry's illustrated version of Thomas Hariot's "Briefe and True Report of the New Found Land of Virginia" (1590).

In 1967, scholars determined that Jacques Le Moyne de Morgues (1533–1588) painted the miniature—an artist who accompanied a French expedition to northern Florida in 1564. As the group's cartographer and illustrator, Le Moyne drew the local plants, animals, and native Timucuan people. During this failed venture to establish a colony, Le Moyne's drawings were destroyed in an attack by the Spanish—who wanted their own colony there—yet his images survived as models for the engravings in de Bry's second volume of the "Briefe and True Report." Le Moyne became known for his botanical drawings, yet died before he could publish his version of the expedition. His widow sold his paintings to de Bry, who altered those images with his son to suit the market. White's and Le Moyne's images, their factuality suspect, remain significant because they are among the earliest European depictions of the New World.

In all this historical confusion and colonial violence, with all these daughters, who is the Pict Daughter? To the European fantasies of sexy, native women, whitewashed and available through time and space, this painting adds yet another layer of incongruity. Early Britons, the Picts dwelled in modern-day Scotland during the Iron Age and Early Medieval periods. *Picti* means "painted or tattooed people," as they were known in legends for painting themselves in battle. (And, St. Ninian was the Apostle to the Southern Picts.)

White's copy of the Pict Woman sports astronomical and geometrical tattoos, instead of floral ones. Le Moyne's version exacerbates its unreliability by decorating her with botanicals introduced to Western Europe, according to Lisa Ford for the Yale Center for British Art, who writes, "The Pictish illustrations were intended to remind readers that early natives of the British Isles existed in a savage state similar to natives in the Americas." With no True Report and faced with these erasures and projections, the Young Daughter strides out of this representational enigma and remains to me witty and captivating. Out of this infinity of copies and in the tradition of ekphrastic prosopopoeia—making the art talk in the poem—I wanted to let her speak for herself.

I modeled the questions in "Dating Profile" from the list on OkCupid. Hieronymus Bosch painted *The Garden of Earthly Delights* between 1495–1505.

In "Come Back!," I refer to "The Walls Do Not Fall," the first long poem of H.D.'s *Trilogy* (1944). In the area of upstate New York and southwestern Vermont where I have lived the past twelve years, the chemical PFOA, dumped by several companies, was discovered in the groundwater in levels that are unsafe for drinking.

I was thinking in "To Bring You News" of this lovely part of William Carlos Williams's poem, "Asphodel, That Greeny Flower":

> My heart rouses
> thinking to bring you news
> of something

that concerns you
    and concerns many men.

In addition to Ashbery's perfect line, I had Angus Fletcher's *Allegory* (1970) in mind while I wrote "Beautiful Poetry." Fletcher taught me that a sestina is a battle of words for dominance. William Butler Yeats's "Leda and the Swan" also stayed in my thoughts: "Being so caught up / So mastered."

ACKNOWLEDGMENTS

At Length: "Family Collection," "My Boyfriend, John Keats";
Boston Review: "Diamonds";
Green Mountains Review: "Girl Twirling";
Interim: A Journal: "I Am Giving Up Poetry," "Magical Object";
The Iowa Review: "A Young Daughter of the Picts," "During the Middle Ages," "The Ideal Form";
The New Republic: "Virgil, Hey";
On the Seawall: "Come Back!," "To Bring You News";
Pleiades: Literature in Context: "Wise Woman";
Poem-a-Day from the Academy of American Poets: "Serious Moonlight";
Poetry Foundation: "Be More Like Björk," "Beautiful Poetry";
Tin House: "Drama Trap" (now titled "Love, Madame du Barry");
The Volta: "Upon Reading Milton";
The White Review: "Beautiful Poetry."

"Beautiful Poetry" appeared in *Another Instance: Jack Collum, Camille Guthrie, Mark McMorris*, edited by Beth Anderson, Elizabeth Robinson, and Laura Sims (Instance Press, 2011).

I read and discussed "Be More Like Björk" for the Poetry Foundation's podcast *PoetryNow*, produced by Michael Slosek and Katie Klocksin (24 April 2017).

"Virgil, Hey" was included in *The Best American Poetry 2019*, edited by Major Jackson; series editor, David Lehman (Scribner, 2019).

"During the Middle Ages" appeared in *The Best American Poetry 2020*, edited by Paisley Rekdal; series editor, David Lehman (Scribner, 2020).

I read several poems from this book for *Poetry Spoken Here*, a podcast series curated by Charlie Rossiter (Episode #117, February 2020).

The Long Devotion: Poets Writing Motherhood, edited by Emily Pérez and Nancy Reddy, reprinted "Virgil, Hey" (University of Georgia Press, 2021).

I'm truly grateful to the editors who published poems from this book: Beth Anderson, Erin Adair-Hodges, Izzy Casey, Alex Dimitrov, Timothy Donnelly, Camille T. Dungy, Jonathan Farmer, Regan Good, Stefania Heim, Cathy Park Hong, Major Jackson, Claudia Keelan, Karla Kelsey, David Lehman, Jenny Molberg, Emily Pérez, Elizabeth Powell, Nancy Reddy, Paisley Rekdal, Elizabeth Robinson, Laura Sims, Ron Slate, Michael Slosek, Devon Walker-Figueroa, Joshua Marie Wilkinson, and Winniebell Xinyu Zong. Many thanks to the poet and journalist Alissa Quart who wrote about my poems in *The Guardian*.

My heartfelt thanks to Peter Conners for choosing my book and for inviting me to be a part of the history of BOA Editions—and to the entire BOA team for their support, warmth, and skill: Ron Martin-Dent, Sandy Knight, Daphne Morrissey, Genevieve Hartman, Richard Foerster, Aimee Conners, Jennifer Rampe, and Zack Gilbert.

My gratitude to the Yaddo Foundation and to Elaina Richardson for the blissful time to begin these poems. I am also very thankful to MacDowell for a residency to complete this book in the Kirby cabin among the pines.

I am indebted to my brilliant friends and colleagues who read these poems, gave excellent advice, and offered encouraging words: Brooke Allen, Ben Anastas, Julianna Baggott, Sally Ball, April Bernard, Tina Cane, Michael Dumanis, Magdalena Edwards,

Marguerite Feitlowitz, Jessica Fisher, Carmen Giménez-Smith, Stefania Heim, Rage Hezekiah, Ann Lauterbach, Jacki Lyden, Erika Meitner, Katie Peterson, Eléna Rivera, Mary Ruefle, Michael Scharf, Russell Switzer, Phillip B. Williams, Emily Wilson, and Mark Wunderlich.

Especial thanks to B.K. Fischer for her generous camaraderie.

Laura Sims, thank you for your friendship, help, and cheer in this writing life.

Donna Stonecipher, I am grateful for that day we met in college. Thank you for your belief in my poems.

To my wonderful friends, who carried me through this time, my affectionate thanks: Shannon Barsotti, J Blackwell, Connie Brooks, Rebecca Brooks, Chris Callahan, Andrew Cencini, Phoebe Cohen, H.S. Cross, Thorsten Dennerline, Jason Dolmetsch, Gretchen Dwyer, Maria Fahey, Bianca Grimshaw, Sarah Harris, Kiaran Honderich, Alexina Jones, Meg Kroeplin, Amie Jo McClellan, Erin McKenny, Erika Mijlin, Ann Pibal, Daisy Rockwell, Betsy Sherman, Debbie Warnock, Beth Wallace, Oceana Wilson, and Aaron York.

I am deeply grateful for my loving family and for my charming, hilarious children.

My love and my gratitude, finally, to Andrew McIntyre.

ABOUT THE AUTHOR

Camille Guthrie is the author of three previous collections of poetry: *Articulated Lair: Poems for Louise Bourgeois* (2013), *In Captivity* (2006), and *The Master Thief* (2000)—all published by Subpress. Her poems have appeared in such publications as *At Length, Boston Review, The Iowa Review, The New Republic, Poem-a-Day, Tin House*, as well as in several anthologies including *The Best American Poetry 2019* & *2020* (Scribner) and *Art & Artists: Poems* (Everyman's Library). She holds an MFA from Brown University and a BA from Vassar College, and she has been awarded fellowships from MacDowell and the Yaddo Foundation. Currently, she is the Director of Undergraduate Writing Initiatives at Bennington College. Born in Seattle, she moved to Pittsburgh at twelve, then later lived in Brooklyn for many years. Now she lives in rural Vermont with her two children.

BOA EDITIONS, LTD.,
AMERICAN POETS CONTINUUM SERIES

No. 1 *The Fuhrer Bunker: A Cycle of Poems in Progress*
W. D. Snodgrass

No. 2 *She*
M. L. Rosenthal

No. 3 *Living With Distance*
Ralph J. Mills, Jr.

No. 4 *Not Just Any Death*
Michael Waters

No. 5 *That Was Then: New and Selected Poems*
Isabella Gardner

No. 6 *Things That Happen Where There Aren't Any People*
William Stafford

No. 7 *The Bridge of Change: Poems 1974–1980*
John Logan

No. 8 *Signatures*
Joseph Stroud

No. 9 *People Live Here: Selected Poems 1949–1983*
Louis Simpson

No. 10 *Yin*
Carolyn Kizer

No. 11 *Duhamel: Ideas of Order in Little Canada*
Bill Tremblay

No. 12 *Seeing It Was So*
Anthony Piccione

No. 13 *Hyam Plutzik: The Collected Poems*

No. 14 *Good Woman: Poems and a Memoir 1969–1980*
Lucille Clifton

No. 15 *Next: New Poems*
Lucille Clifton

No. 16 *Roxa: Voices of the Culver Family*
William B. Patrick

No. 17 *John Logan: The Collected Poems*

No. 18 *Isabella Gardner: The Collected Poems*

No. 19 *The Sunken Lightship*
Peter Makuck

No. 20 *The City in Which I Love You*
Li-Young Lee

No. 21 *Quilting: Poems 1987–1990*
Lucille Clifton

No. 22 *John Logan: The Collected Fiction*

No. 23 *Shenandoah and Other Verse Plays*
Delmore Schwartz

No. 24 *Nobody Lives on Arthur Godfrey Boulevard*
Gerald Costanzo

No. 25 *The Book of Names: New and Selected Poems*
Barton Sutter

No. 26 *Each in His Season*
W. D. Snodgrass

No. 27 *Wordworks: Poems Selected and New*
Richard Kostelanetz

No. 28 *What We Carry*
Dorianne Laux

No. 29 *Red Suitcase*
Naomi Shihab Nye

No. 30 *Song*
Brigit Pegeen Kelly

No. 31 *The Fuehrer Bunker: The Complete Cycle*
W. D. Snodgrass

COLOPHON

BOA Editions, Ltd., a not-for-profit publisher of poetry
and other literary works, fosters readership and appreciation
of contemporary literature. By identifying, cultivating, and
publishing both new and established poets and selecting authors
of unique literary talent, BOA brings high-quality literature
to the public. Support for this effort comes from the sale of its
publications, grant funding, and private donations.

The publication of this book is made possible, in part,
by the support of the following individuals:

Anonymous (x3)
Nelson Adrian Blish
Gary & Gwen Conners
Charles & Danielle Coté
The Chris Dahl & Ruth Rowse Charitable Fund
Bonnie Garner
Robert & Rae Gilson
Margaret Heminway
Grant Holcomb
Kathleen C. Holcombe
Nora A. Jones
Paul LaFerriere & Dorrie Parini
John & Barbara Lovenheim
Melanie & Ron Martin-Dent
Joe McElveney
Sherry Phillips & Richard Margolis Donor Advised Fund
Boo Poulin
Deborah Ronnen
Elizabeth Spenst
William Waddell & Linda Rubel
Bruce & Jean Weigl
Glenn & Helen William